RUSSIA
the culture

Greg Nickles

A Bobbie Kalman Book

The Lands, Peoples, and Cultures Series

 Crabtree Publishing Company

www.crabtreebooks.com

The Lands, Peoples, and Cultures Series

Created by Bobbie Kalman

Coordinating editor
Ellen Rodger

Project development, editing, and design
First Folio Resource Group, Inc.
Pauline Beggs
Tom Dart
Kathryn Lane
Alana Perez
Debbie Smith

Separations and film
Dot 'n Line Image Inc.

Printer
Worzalla Publishing Company

Consultants
Theodore H. Friedgut; Larissa Kisseleva-van Amsterdam; Bella Kotik-Friedgut; Evgueni Petrusevich, Consulate General, Russian Federation, Montreal; Sergei Ulianitsky; and Paul van Amsterdam

Photographs
Beniaminson/Art Resource, NY: p. 14 (right); Corbis/AFP: p. 12 (top); Corbis/Tiziana and Gianni Baldizzone: p. 17 (bottom); Corbis/Dave Bartruff: p. 11; Corbis/Bettmann: p. 23 (bottom), p. 26, p. 28 (top); Corbis/Bojan Brecelj: p. 24 (top), Robert Eric/Corbis Sygma/Magma p. 25 (top); Corbis / Magma / Earl & Nazima Kowall, p. 25 (bottom) Corbis/Diego Lezama Orezzoli: p. 18 (right); Corbis/José F. Poblete: p. 27 (top left); Corbis/Enzo and Paolo Ragazzini: cover; Corbis/Steve Raymer: p. 10 (bottom right), p. 23 (top); Corbis/Gregor Schmid: title page; Corbis/Micheal T. Sedam: p. 3; Express Newspapers/Archive Photos: p. 13; Giraudon/Art Resource, NY: p. 21 (bottom right); Sylvain Grandadam/Photo Researchers: p. 20 (left); Jeff Greenberg/Photo Researchers: p. 27 (top right); George Holton/Photo Researchers: p. 22 (top); Andy Johnstone/Impact: p. 27 (bottom); Wolfgang Kaehler: p. 8, p. 9 (left and top right), p. 10 (left), p. 16 (both), p. 18 (left), p. 19 (top), p. 20 (right), p. 22 (bottom); Erich Lessing/Art Resource, NY: p. 7 (both); Fred Maroon/Photo Researchers: p. 5; Nimatallah/Art Resource, NY: p. 15 (bottom right); Popperfoto/ Archive Photos: p. 21 (left); Reuters/Yuri Gripas/ Archive Photos: p. 9 (bottom right); Reuters/Pawel Kopczynski/Archive Photos: p. 24 (bottom); Reuters/ Alexander Natruskin/Archive Photos: p. 29 (bottom); Stephen L. Saks/Photo Researchers: p. 17 (top); Scala/Art Resource, NY: p. 4 (both), p. 6 (both), p. 12 (bottom), p. 15 (left and top right), p. 28 (bottom); Snark/Art Resource, NY: p. 14 (left), p. 29 (top); Charles Steiner/International Stock Photo: p. 21 (top right); J. Robert Stottlemyer/International Stock Photo: p. 19 (bottom); Janet Wishnetsky/Impact: p. 10 (top right)

Illustrations
Alexei Mezentsev: pp. 30–31
David Wysotski, Allure Illustrations: back cover

Cover: The Church of the Intercession, on Kizhi Island in northwest Russia, has 22 cupolas and is built entirely out of wood, without a single nail.

Title page: Mother Russia stands 52 meters (170 feet) tall as a memorial to those who died fighting in the city of Volgograd during World War II.

Icon: *Balalaikas*, traditional Russian musical instruments, appear at the head of each section.

Back cover: The Kamchatka brown bear is a symbol of Russia.

Published by
Crabtree Publishing Company

PMB 16A	612 Welland Avenue,	73 Lime Walk
350 Fifth Avenue	St. Catharines,	Headington
Suite 3308	Ontario, Canada	Oxford OX3 7AD
New York	L2M 5V6	United Kingdom
N.Y. 10118		

Cataloging in Publication Data
Nickles, Greg 1969-
    Russia--the culture / Greg Nickles.
    p.cm.-- (The lands, peoples, and cultures series)
    Includes index.
    Summary: Text and photos show how Russians celebrate holidays and festivals, using art, music, and dance.
    ISBN 0-86505-240-9 (RLB) -- ISBN 0-86505-320-0 (pbk.)
    1. Russia (Federation)--Social life and customs--Juvenile literature.[1. Holidays--Russia (Federation) 2. Festivals--Russia (Federation) 3. Russia (Federation)--Social life and customs.]1. Title.II Series.
    DK510.762.N53 2000
    306'.0947--dc21
                                                99-056187
                                                LC

Contents

Between East and West

Russia is a land with a rich history of **customs**, beliefs, and traditions. For over a thousand years, its people have expressed their creativity through a variety of arts, including painting, crafts, architecture, dance, music, and literature.

Russia lies across two continents with very different cultures — Asia in the east and Europe in the west. Over the centuries, people from each continent introduced their cultures to Russia. Russia's most important thinkers, artists, and writers skillfully combined the ideas of both the East and West with their own.

For much of the twentieth century, the government restricted religion and controlled the arts in Russia. Today, however, Russians are looking to their proud past and to ideas from other countries as they revive their culture.

Carl Fabergé, a jeweler from St. Petersburg, created dazzling egg-shaped art objects which Russian nobles exchanged as gifts. This Fabergé egg was made in 1891 and contains a tiny model of a sailing ship.

(opposite) Massive statues brace the weight of a balcony outside the Hermitage museum in St. Petersburg.

*Vasily Surikov (1848–1916) was one of the **Perevizniki**, or Wanderers. This group of Russian painters organized "wandering," or mobile, exhibitions of their art. They wanted to bring their work to the common people who did not have access to it.*

Culture through the ages

The ancient **ancestors** of the Russians, the East Slavs, lived in Eastern Europe over a thousand years ago. They enjoyed telling stories, singing folk songs, and performing folk dances. They also created many useful, colorfully decorated crafts, clothing, and tools.

Christianity comes to Russia

In 988 A.D., the leader of the East Slavs, Prince Vladimir, chose Christianity as his people's official religion. Christianity is based on the teachings of Jesus Christ, who is believed to be the son of God. **Priests** from the powerful **Byzantine Empire** to the south taught the East Slavs about Christianity. As the people adopted their new religion, they learned Byzantine styles of painting, architecture, and music. They were also introduced to reading and writing.

Mongol rule

In the 1200s, the **Mongol Empire** in the East **invaded** and took control of the East Slavs' lands. During the centuries of their rule, the Mongols allowed the East Slavs to continue most of their religious practices and traditional arts. They also promoted trade and the exchange of ideas between the East Slavs and other parts of the Mongol Empire.

Under the czars

In the 1500s, Russian **emperors** called **czars** defeated the Mongol rulers. Over the next few centuries, many czars, especially Peter the Great, encouraged Russians to adopt new ideas and styles of art from the rest of Europe. They sent Russians to school in other countries and brought foreign artists to work in Russia. The people learned the artistic styles of Western Europe and produced masterpieces of literature, music, dance, and visual arts that had a Russian flavor.

From the thirteenth to sixteenth century, Russia's czars wore crowns such as this one, decorated in the Byzantine style.

(right) Women in traditional cloaks attend church during the 19th century, in a painting by Andreij Riabushkin.

In this painting by Henri Gervex, Nicolas Romanov and Empress Alexandra are being crowned the new czar and czaritza in 1894.

Strict Soviets

In 1917, the last czar, Nicolas II, was overthrown. Russia became part of a new country called the **Soviet** Union that was run by a **Communist** government. The Soviet rulers tightly controlled many areas of Russian life, including culture. They supported great new museums, galleries, and theaters, but they also destroyed priceless artwork and imprisoned, **exiled**, or killed writers whose ideas did not agree with their own. Soviet rulers also discouraged religion, so people often **worshiped** in secret.

Culture revived

In 1991, the Soviet Union split apart and Russia again became its own country. Its new government allows people to worship and express their ideas without fear of punishment. These freedoms have led Russians to rediscover their country's rich culture and create new art in both traditional and modern styles.

In this painting by Vassiliji Chvostenko, Vladimir Ilyich Lenin, the first leader of the Soviet Union, inspires his troops during the October Revolution of 1917.

Religion

Russia's people practice many religions. Most follow the Russian Orthodox Church, a **denomination** of Christianity. Some belong to different Christian churches or follow other religions such as Islam, Judaism, or Buddhism. Young Russians tend to worship only on special occasions or may not believe in religion at all, while some older people go to church every day.

Christianity

The Christian holy book, the Bible, tells about the life and teachings of Jesus Christ and his followers. Christians worship Jesus, the son of God, who they believe performed miracles. One of his greatest miracles was returning to life after he was nailed to a cross and killed for his beliefs. Christians also pray to Jesus' mother, Mary, and other holy people called saints who performed miracles.

Russian Orthodoxy

When Christianity first came to Russia, the **patriarch**, or head priest, of Constantinople led Russia's churches. At that time, Constantinople, which is today the city of Istanbul in Turkey, was the **capital** of the Byzantine Empire. By the 1400s, Russian churches began to follow their own patriarch, who lived in Moscow. After that time, the Russian denomination of Christianity became known as the Russian Orthodox Church.

Many Russian Orthodox churches are filled with icons, which are portraits of saints and other holy people from the Bible.

Outside and inside

Russian Orthodox churches are often octagonal, or eight-sided, and have roofs with onion-shaped domes. Inside, the smoke and scent of burning **incense** floats through the air. Soft daylight and candles light up beautiful golden decorations. An elaborate screen, called an **iconostasis**, stands in front of the altar, where church services are held. During a service, the priest enters and exits the church's main room through the Royal Gates, or special doors in the middle of the iconostasis. There are no pews or other places for worshipers to sit inside a Russian Orthodox church. Instead, they stand or kneel, facing the iconostasis.

(above) Onion-shaped domes sit at the top of spires on many churches in Russia.

(below) The Russian Orthodox patriarch Alexei II sprays holy water over worshipers in a Moscow church.

(above) The Royal Gates, covered in gold and decorated with icons, lead through the iconostasis to the altar.

Other religions

Not all Russians are Christians. About twelve million people are Muslim. They follow the religion of Islam. Islam is based on the teachings of the **prophet** Muhammad who was born in Mecca, in present-day Saudi Arabia. In the far north and east, thousands of people worship the forces of nature. Others believe in Buddhism, a religion started by Buddha, a teacher from India who lived 2500 years ago. There are also hundreds of thousands of Jews throughout Russia, who follow the teachings of their holy book, the Torah.

(above) Jews pray in a synagogue, with their heads covered by a **tallit***, a prayer shawl.*

(top) A Muslim couple read from the Qur'an, the holy book of Islam.

(left) In a brightly painted Buddhist temple, monks chant the teachings of Buddha.

Holidays and festivals

The Russian calendar is filled with holidays and other special occasions. The most important events are based on the Russian Orthodox Church's holy days. These days are observed with religious services, **fasts**, feasts, and parties.

A girl shows off her beautifully decorated Easter eggs.

The Easter festival

The Easter festival, which marks the death of Jesus Christ and his return to life, is held in early spring. Easter is the most important Christian holiday. Russian Orthodox Christians fast in the weeks before Easter Sunday. They begin with one week of "Butter Fast," during which they give up meat. Butter Fast ends with a feast of *blini*. These thin pancakes are served with heaps of sour cream and butter, and are rolled around fish or caviar, a salty delicacy made from fish eggs.

Lent and the Easter service

After the *blini* feast, a period of six weeks, called Lent, begins. During Lent, many people give up meat, dairy products, and fish. They eat only vegetables and use only vegetable oil. Lent ends after an all-night church service that begins on the eve of Easter. During this service, people walk around the church holding candles and crosses, a symbol of Christianity, as their priest leads them in prayer.

Easter feasting

Easter is a day of feasting. At each meal, people eat rich foods that were not allowed during Lent. The most important of the many dishes are the *pascha*, a pyramid of cream cheese with nuts and dried fruit, and the *kulich*, or fruit breads that look like small towers. People sometimes take these dishes to the church so that the priest can bless them. People also eat hard-boiled eggs, colorfully painted for the Easter feast. A common custom is for each person to crack their eggshell against a neighbor's, then eat their egg as an **appetizer**.

The Yuletide season

Christmas and New Year's are part of a season of merrymaking called Yuletide. Christmas celebrates the birth of Christ. It is a fairly quiet, religious holiday that was discouraged during Soviet times. Instead, the government encouraged people to celebrate New Year's. In the late 1980s and early 1990s, however, people slowly began to celebrate Christmas again. When Soviet rule ended in 1991, Christmas became a national holiday.

Yuletide feasts

In the weeks before Christmas, some people fast. When the first star appears on Christmas Eve, the fast is broken. Families eat a sweet, traditional dish called *kutija*. *Kutija* is made of rice or cooked whole wheat mixed with walnuts, raisins, and honey. Then, they set the table for a large supper. After dining on goose or duck, ham, sweets, and tea, many families sing old Russian carols called *kolyadi*. These short, happy songs are accompanied by cheerful wishes for good health, good fortune, and good crops for the coming year. Carolers also visit other people's homes, singing and scattering plant seeds as a symbol of a good summer harvest. In return, they receive sweets or a coin before continuing to the next home.

(left) Men dressed as Grandfather Frost travel on the Moscow subway to their jobs in department stores.

(below) The Snow Maiden stands among startled villagers, in this painting from the lid of a box.

What is the date?

In 46 B.C., Julius Caesar, leader of the **Roman Empire**, changed the calendar to keep better track of time. His Julian calendar was used throughout Europe until 1582, when the leader of the Roman Catholic Church, Pope Gregory XIII, replaced it with the Gregorian calendar. The Gregorian calendar was shorter than the Julian calendar, so holidays fell on different dates. For example, Christmas moved from January 7 to December 25. Although many countries adopted the Gregorian calendar immediately, Russia did not until 1918. The Russian Orthodox Church, however, still uses the old Julian calendar and celebrates Christmas on January 7.

Mixed traditions

During Soviet times, many Christmas symbols became part of New Year's celebrations. For example, the Christmas tree became the New Year's tree and Saint Nicholas became Grandfather Frost. Today, people still celebrate New Year's with a tree and with gifts from Grandfather Frost and his granddaughter, the Snow Maiden. Often, Grandfather Frost and the Snow Maiden give out these presents after special holiday plays in which they outsmart wicked storybook characters. New Year's celebrations also include a feast. It begins at the last stroke of midnight on New Year's Eve, often by cracking open a bottle of **champagne**.

May Day, on the first of May, was once a huge holiday to honor workers. Thousands of people marched in Moscow's Red Square, carrying banners with photos of state heroes and leaders. Today, it is a much smaller event.

Other events

Russians observe other holidays throughout the year. March 8, International Women's Day, celebrates working women. On this day, men bring women beautiful bouquets of tulips and snowdrops, and do the housework that women usually do. On Victory Day, in early May, people remember the millions of Russians who died during World War II, which was fought in Russia between 1941 and 1945. War **veterans** wear their medals in public and people place wreaths on war monuments. Independence Day, on June 12, is the newest holiday. It celebrates Russia's independence from the Soviet Union.

Russian art

Russia's rich tradition of art stretches back many centuries. It includes religious paintings, modern art, and film. In the twentieth century, the Soviet government wanted artists to produce paintings and sculptures that portrayed happy citizens and wise leaders. The leaders hoped this artwork would convince people to be content with their difficult daily lives.

Some artists who refused to paint what the Soviet government wanted were not allowed to display their work in government-funded galleries. They worked in secret, showing their paintings and sculptures to only a few trusted friends. Today, artists no longer need to work in secret. They are creating many new and exciting pieces of art that are exhibited in galleries across the country and around the world.

Soldiers show their allegiance to the Communist party in a 1918 poster meant to encourage people to support the Communists.

Sacred art

One of Russia's oldest styles of artwork is religious portraits. A thousand years ago, Russian artists were trained by Byzantine painters to create frescoes, or paintings done on church walls while the plaster was still wet. They also created **icons**, which were painted on wood. They used soft, rich colors, gold leaf, and detailed patterns. At the time, the Church did not want artists to create realistic sculptures or paintings because it feared that people might worship them, so portraits were not lifelike.

An icon, or religious painting, shows Mary with the baby Jesus.

(opposite) Natalia Goncharova (1881–1962) was an important painter, sculptor, and stage designer. She created paintings like "Gathering Wood."

Western and modern art

In the seventeenth century, under Czar Peter the Great, Russians began to create realistic paintings and sculptures, including portraits of leaders and landowners, peasant lifestyles, and landscapes. In the early twentieth century, Russia was the birthplace of some of the world's most celebrated modern artists, including Wassily Kandinsky and Marc Chagall. Kandinsky was a pioneer of abstract art, a style that does not try to look realistic. Chagall was inspired by myths and Russian folk art. Film also became a popular art form in the twentieth century. Russians were pioneers in making movies that portrayed history's great heroes and events.

(right) Wassily Kandinsky created swirling paintings, such as "Two Ovals," painted in 1919.

(below) Marc Chagall created dreamlike paintings, such as "The Grey House," in 1917.

Folk arts

For centuries, Russian artisans, or craftspeople, have made all sorts of folk art, including clothing, toys, and household decorations. They have used both ordinary and uncommon materials, such as wood, wool, clay, bone, and bark, in their work and have passed their skills down from generation to generation.

Fabric arts

Creating artwork out of fabric is a very popular pastime. People weave, sew, knit, and make lace by hand. They add beadwork and embroidery, or detailed designs made with colorful thread, to traditional clothing, napkins, tablecloths, and wall hangings. When clothes and other fabrics wear out, people tear them into strips and knot them together to make carpets and rugs.

(above) In northern Siberia, people decorate ceremonial clothing with colorful beadwork.

(left) People who live in the countryside decorate the windows and eaves of their homes with intricately carved wood trim.

From wood

Wood is one of the most common materials for making crafts in Russia, since it is plentiful and inexpensive. Artisans make wooden animals, puppets, dolls, games, and boxes that they later hand-paint with beautiful scenes from fairy tales. They also create traditional wooden tools, furniture, or utensils, such as the *kovsh*, a ladle carved in the shape of a duck.

Matryoshkas

One of the most popular examples of Russian folk art is the *matryoshka*, a set of seven dolls that fit inside one another. *Matryoshkas* are made of wood and coated with lacquer, a shiny, clear varnish. They are traditionally painted in bright colors to look like women wearing kerchiefs and dresses. Other designs, such as Christmas characters, cartoons of Soviet rulers, and even North American basketball players, are also popular. *Matryoshkas* are a favorite with tourists and are **exported** all over the world.

(below) An artist carefully paints icons and scenes from fairy tales on wooden boxes.

Matryoshkas *sit on display at an outdoor market. Can you spot the set of czars? What about a famous British pop group?*

Architecture

Russia has many beautiful and unique buildings that reflect different styles of architecture. Some of the oldest buildings are in Moscow, Russia's capital. St. Petersburg, to the north, is home to more modern Russian treasures, built by Peter the Great and later czars. The Soviet government also constructed impressive buildings throughout the country.

At the center of St. Basil's Cathedral, a pointed tower stands 33 meters (107 feet) tall, capped by a small golden cupola and cross.

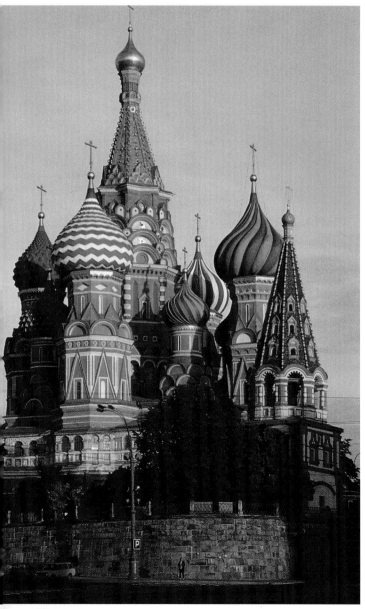

Byzantine style

The Byzantine style strongly influenced early Russian architecture. At first, Russians copied the design of Byzantine churches, which included towers capped by golden **cupolas**, or domes. Gradually, architects changed the style to suit Russian tastes. They added colors, more cupolas, and smaller windows to keep out cold winds. They also made the cupolas more pointed, or onion-shaped. This shape resembled the shape of domes on mosques, Muslim houses of worship. It also had the advantage of allowing snow to slide off easily.

St. Basil's Cathedral

The Cathedral of St. Basil the Blessed, also known as St. Basil's Cathedral, is located in the heart of Moscow. It was completed in 1561, during the reign of Czar Ivan the Terrible, and has become one of the most famous buildings in the world. It is said that after the cathedral was completed, Ivan the Terrible ordered that its architects be blinded so they would never be able to create another, more beautiful church.

*Many cupolas are covered with carefully overlapped wooden shingles, called **lemekhi**.*

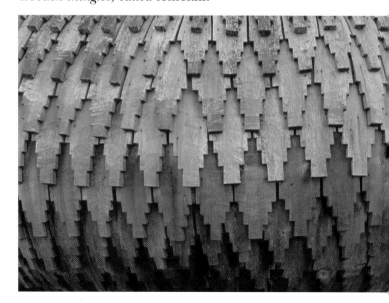

Russia's rulers do not live in the Winter Palace any more. It is now part of a world-famous art gallery called the Hermitage, a place that everyone can enjoy.

Peter's city

In 1703, Czar Peter the Great ordered the construction of a new city — St. Petersburg. Peter wanted his city, which replaced Moscow as Russia's capital from 1713 to 1917, to have buildings as beautiful as those in France, the most powerful and stylish country of the day. St. Petersburg's elegant buildings, decorated with sculptures, set an example for future Russian architecture.

The Winter Palace

Later rulers built one of St. Petersburg's most beautiful structures. The Winter Palace has over a thousand rooms, including grand ballrooms, dining halls, bed chambers, a church, and a richly decorated throne room made of bronze and colored marble. Outside are beautiful gardens, bronze sculptures, and the tall Alexander Column, which honors the 1812 military victory of Czar Alexander I over the French emperor, Napoleon Bonaparte.

Soviet styles

Among the most famous buildings in Russia are seven lavish towers in Moscow, including the Hotel Ukraine and Moscow State University. These buildings, which were built during the Soviet era, have many stepped levels stacked on top of one another. Foreign tourists have nicknamed the buildings "wedding cakes." The Soviet government also built gorgeous marble and metal subway stations filled with artwork and chandeliers. Most other Soviet buildings, however, were constructed as quickly as possible with little decoration, using inexpensive materials such as concrete.

Moscow State University is a huge, imposing building.

Music

Russians play and listen to all sorts of music. They have composed some of the world's most famous symphonies and operas. They also have rich church and folk music traditions, as well as a love of jazz and rock.

Russian folk music

Byliny songs are old folk songs that are partly spoken. Some are over a thousand years old! These songs tell the stories of great heroes, evil villains, and fantastic deeds. They were once performed by peasants or professional entertainers who made their living traveling from town to town. Today, they are sung by many other Russians.

A folk group, including an accordion player and a **balalaika** *player, perform in a St. Petersburg park.*

A woman in traditional costume sings folk songs in Moscow.

The Western tradition

Russian **composers** of the nineteenth and twentieth centuries are some of the most famous composers in the world. They created masterpieces for the symphony, opera, and ballet, using traditional Russian folk tales and folk songs as their inspiration. One of the country's best-known composers was Peter Tchaikovsky. His exciting *1812 Overture*, which celebrates Russia's military defeat of the French, even includes cannon blasts!

Peter Tchaikovsky created music for **The Nutcracker,** *a famous Christmas ballet that tells the story of a magical nutcracker soldier.*

Musical pioneers

In the early twentieth century, Russians such as Igor Stravinsky became pioneers of modern music by writing powerful and controversial pieces such as *The Rite of Spring.* Later famous composers include Sergei Prokofiev, who is known for *Peter and the Wolf.* This musical story uses different instruments to portray the characters a young boy meets during his adventures.

In the early 20th century, Igor Stravinsky composed music that sounded strange to many people. His music greatly influenced later composers.

A street musician plays classical music for passers-bys on his French horn.

Folk dance and ballet

Dance is one of the most widely respected arts in Russia. People have enjoyed folk dances for centuries, while ballet was introduced to Russia more recently. Many Russians dance for enjoyment, but others dance professionally and are known throughout the world.

Folk dance

For centuries, Russians have performed folk dances at weddings, parties, country fairs, and other celebrations. Many of these dances tell stories of village life and Russian customs. Couples dressed in brightly embroidered costumes dance to fast melodies played on traditional instruments. Women usually move with smooth, gliding motions, while men stomp their feet to the beat of the music and run to make high kicks and jumps. Sometimes their foot stomping gets so fast and furious that they break a heel off their boots!

Folk dancers perform in a Moscow theater.

At a hunter's festival in eastern Siberia, dancers move to the beat of drums.

(above) Ballet students stretch at the bar.

(left) Mikhail Baryshnikov leaps high into the air during a dress rehearsal in New York City. The United States became his home after he left the Soviet Union.

Ballet

The ballet is Russia's most famous form of dance. It came to the country over 270 years ago, when Czaritza Anna, who ruled from 1730 to 1740, and Czaritza Elizabeth, who ruled from 1741 to 1762, brought teachers from France to train dancers for their royal court. Before long, independent troupes, or companies of dancers, were performing throughout the country. By the mid-1800s, Russian dancers and composers were creating some of the most stunning ballets in the world, with elegant jumps and turns, beautiful costumes, and elaborate sets.

Rising stars

Ballet dancers begin training at a very young age. Talented children attend special schools, where they learn ballet in addition to subjects such as science and history. Young dancers dream of performing for the best of Russia's many dance companies — the Kirov-Maryinsky Ballet of St. Petersburg or the Bolshoi Ballet of Moscow.

Unfortunately, Russia lost some of its best modern ballet dancers during Soviet times. Performers such as Natalia Makarova, Mikhail Baryshnikov, and Rudolf Nureyev left for other countries, where they believed they would lead a better life.

 # The circus

For more than two centuries, Russian adults and children have enjoyed some of the world's best circus acts. Each year, Russian circus troupes tour the country, ensuring that millions of people, even those in remote towns, get to see their shows. The best-known troupes, such as the Moscow State Circus, regularly tour the world. Russian performers also star in other countries' circuses.

A long tradition

In the late eighteenth century, Czaritza Catherine the Great introduced circus arts to Russia. She invited a famous Englishman, Charles Hughes, to bring his performing horses to St. Petersburg. There, he set up a school for horseback-riding tricks. Hughes and his troupe became so popular that circus arts began to spread throughout the country. The circus was also very popular with the rulers of the Soviet Union, who built excellent schools to train thousands of new performers.

(top) Performers check their form in the wall-sized mirrors at a training center.

Assistants lace up Masza the skating bear's skates just before a performance.

Under the "big top"

Sometimes, Russian troupes perform under a large tent, nicknamed the "big top." Many cities have permanent circus buildings, complete with rehearsal spaces, open air and indoor cages for animals, and comfortable dressing rooms. The troupes often travel in trailers or by train with helpers such as electricians and animal handlers.

In Russian circuses, clowns perform silly acrobatics, riders do daring leaps and headstands on horseback, and trapeze artists flip and spin high above the ground. Some of the audience's favorite performers are the trained dogs, bears, elephants, monkeys, and even hedgehogs!

Schools and sawdust

Many of Russia's circus performers "grow up in the sawdust." Their parents are also circus performers who train them in a real circus ring where the ground is often covered with sawdust. Some Russian families have passed on their skills in this way for generations. Other future circus performers train at professional circus schools. From the age of eleven to seventeen, they study balance and body movement. They also take lessons in specific circus skills such as juggling, clowning, tight-rope walking, or flying on the trapeze. Once students master their skills, they graduate and look for work with a professional troupe.

(top) A lion tamer in the ring with eight male lions at a Moscow Circus performance in Hong Kong, China.

(top) An acrobat leans on a horse at a winter water circus. Russian performers travel the world to work in circus acts.

Writing Russian

People from over 130 different **ethnic groups** live in Russia. Each group has its own language, but almost everyone also speaks Russian, the country's official language. A few Russian words, such as vodka and czar, have become part of the English language.

Cyril's alphabet

The Russian language evolved from Old Slavonic, a language spoken over a thousand years ago by the East Slavs. There was no way of writing Old Slavonic until two monks, Christian men who devote their lives to the Church, invented a special alphabet in the tenth century.

The monks, named Cyril and Methodius, adapted their alphabet from letters in ancient Latin, Greek, and Hebrew. Then, they used their alphabet to translate the Bible. Today, the Cyrillic alphabet, named after Cyril, is used to write Russian and many related languages such as Ukrainian and Serbian. Old Slavonic is still used, but only by priests in the Russian Orthodox Church.

The Cyrillic alphabet

The Cyrillic alphabet has 33 letters. Some look like English letters, but many do not. The sounds of letters that look the same in Russian and English are often quite different. For example, the letter "H" in Russian makes the sound of the English letter "N."

English	Russian	
Hello	Zdrah'stvooite	Здравствуйте
Good morning	Do'braye oo'tra	Доброе утро
Good evening	Do'bree ve'cher	Добрый вечер
Yes	Da	Да
No	Nyet	Нет
Maybe	Mo'zhet byt	Может быть
I beg your pardon?	Prastee'te?	Простите?
Please	Pazhah'lsta	Пожалуйста
Thank you	Spasee'ba	Спасибо
Today	Sevo'dnya	Сегодня
Tomorrow	Zah'ftra	Завтра
Yesterday	Vchera'	Вчера
Stop!	Stop!	Стоп!

(right) **Pravda** *was the Soviet Union's major newspaper from 1918 until 1991, when the Soviet Union collapsed. This front page, from 1961, reports on the firing of a Soviet space probe toward Venus.*

26

(left) In an elaborate icon, Saints Cyril and Methodius hold the Cyrillic alphabet.

(below) People in Moscow read the day's news from cases displaying pages from newspapers.

Popular North American magazines keep their English titles, while the pages are filled with Cyrillic writing.

Literature and drama

Russia has a rich tradition of writing and folklore. Its oldest tales of great battles and princes inspired later authors and poets. Many writers are so respected that monuments have been built in their honor throughout the country.

Russia's great writers

The masterpieces of Russian literature were written in the nineteenth century, beginning with the works of Alexander Pushkin (1799–1837). Pushkin became the country's favorite author of emotional poems about love and honor. He also wrote children's fairy tales in verse that are still very popular today.

Pushkin's great works were followed by those of many masters. Fyodor Dostoyevsky (1821–1881) wrote novels, including his masterpiece *The Brothers Karamazov*, that portray characters who struggle with the ideas of good and evil. Leo Tolstoy (1828–1910) wrote one of the greatest novels of all time, *War and Peace*, about Russia's war in 1812 with the French.

(left) Leo Tolstoy's masterpiece **Anna Karenina** *is a novel about the tragic love affair of a Russian princess.*

(below) Scenes from Alexander Pushkin's tale "On the Seashore" decorate a lacquer box.

Anton Checkhov reads one of his plays to some friends.

At the theater

Russians often go to plays, which cost very little to attend. The country's most famous playwright is Anton Checkhov (1860–1904). Checkhov was a country doctor whose work, including *The Cherry Orchard* and *Uncle Vanya*, focuses on Russian life at the end of the nineteenth century. Pushkin and many other Russian novelists are also known for their plays.

Soviet rules

During Soviet times, the government would not allow authors to write about the country's troubles. Several authors ignored these rules and became famous for their books about the problems that Russia's people faced. The most famous author of this period is Alexander Solzhenitsyn. Solzhenitsyn won the Nobel Prize for literature in 1970, but was thrown out of the country for disobeying the government. He returned to Russia as a hero in 1994.

Alexander Solzhenitsyn was falsely accused of a crime, arrested, and sent to a labor camp for eight years. His novels reflect the terrible experiences he had while in prison.

Enthusiastic readers

Russia has a very high literacy rate, which means that almost everyone can read and write. Russians love books, magazines, and newspapers. In Soviet times, Russians were not allowed to read publications from other countries since the government did not want them to learn about ideas with which it disagreed. Today, Russians can choose from thousands of new magazines and newspapers published in their country and around the world.

A Russian folk tale

Russians like to tell their children fairy tales of heroes, dragons, witches, and magical animals. One popular character is Baba Yaga, an evil witch. Here is a story about Baba Yaga that you can tell a younger brother, sister, or friend.

A tale of Baba Yaga

Natasha lived in a cottage with her father and stepmother. Her stepmother was very cruel. One day, while the father was away, she decided to get rid of Natasha for good.

"Girl," she ordered, "Go to my sister's house and fetch me a needle and thread." Natasha shivered because the sister was the terrible Baba Yaga. No child ever returned from her house! Natasha's stepmother cackled, handed her a bit of cheese wrapped in a kerchief for lunch, and forced her out the door.

Before long, Natasha came to Baba Yaga's yard. There, she met a guard dog who whined from loneliness. Natasha scratched him behind the ears, and he muttered a gruff "Thank you." Next, she met Baba Yaga's servant, who was weeping. Natasha gave her the kerchief to wipe her tears. The servant cheered up and led her to the house.

Natasha gasped when she saw Baba Yaga's strange home. Her house walked around on huge chicken legs! When it bent down to greet them, Natasha saw Baba Yaga standing at the door. Natasha asked her for the needle and thread. Baba Yaga smiled ghoulishly, flashing her iron teeth, and brought her servant and Natasha inside.

"Sit here at my loom, child," Baba Yaga drooled. "While you weave, I'll fetch your thread and needle. My servant will wash your face and comb your hair." Then, she left the room. Natasha did not trust Baba Yaga, and wove nervously at the noisy loom.

Noticing the witch's hungry cat, Natasha offered it her piece of cheese, which it gobbled up. The cat was very grateful and whispered, "Little girl, you must leave. Baba Yaga is going to eat you!" "How can I escape?" Natasha asked, frightened. "I will take your place at the loom," offered the cat, "so she will hear it rattle and think you are still working." The cat started to weave.

"Take my comb and towel," instructed the servant. "Run away, and throw them on the ground when Baba Yaga chases you."

As Natasha slipped out the door, she met the guard dog, who gruffly wished her "Good luck." Then, she ran. When Baba Yaga returned moments later, she discovered the trick.

"Why did you help her escape?" she screamed at her cat, servant, and dog. "You never gave me a scrap to eat," said the cat, "but she gave me cheese!" "You never gave me a penny," said the servant, "but she gave me a beautiful kerchief!" "You never paid any attention to me," said the dog, "but she scratched my head!"

Baba Yaga cursed them and hopped onto her flying **mortar** and **pestle**, which she also used to pound bones into dust. When she caught up to Natasha, the little girl threw down her towel. Suddenly, it turned into a raging river which Baba Yaga could not fly over. Furious, Baba Yaga found a herd of cattle and drove them into the river, commanding them to drink. Once they finished the last drop, she again started flying toward Natasha. Then, the girl threw down the comb, which grew into a thick forest. Unable to see through the dark trees, Baba Yaga cursed and gave up the chase.

When Natasha got home, she found her father crying. He had learned about the trip to Baba Yaga's and chased away the evil stepmother forever. Together, Natasha and her father lived happily ever after.

Glossary

ancestor A person from whom one is descended

appetizer Food served before the main course

Byzantine Empire An empire that existed from 395, when the Roman Empire was divided, to 1453. During the sixth century, it included Turkey, Greece, Italy, and parts of northern Africa and Spain.

capital A city where the government of a state or country is located

champagne A bubbly wine made in the region of Champagne, in France, which people often drink for celebrations

Communist A person who believes in an economic system where the country's natural resources, businesses, and industry are owned and controlled by the government

composer A person who writes music

cupola A dome

custom Something that a group of people has done for so long that it becomes an important part of their way of life

czar The title given to Russian emperors

denomination An organized religious group within a faith

emperor A ruler of a country or group of countries

empire A group of countries or territories having the same ruler

ethnic group A group of people who share a common race, language, heritage, or religion

exile To force someone to leave a country or home

export To sell goods to another country

fast The act of not eating any food or certain kinds of food for religious or health reasons

incense A substance that is burned to create a pleasant smell

icon A holy picture of Jesus Christ, an angel, a saint, or another important person in Christianity

iconostasis A screen covered in icons that stands in front of the altar in an Eastern Orthodox church

invade To enter using force

Mongol Empire An empire formed in the thirteenth century which stretched from China to Europe and included parts of Russia

mortar A bowl for crushing things with a pestle

patriarch The head of the Russian Orthodox Church

pestle A tool with a rounded end that is used to crush things into a powder, usually in a mortar

priest A religious leader

prophet A person who is believed to speak on behalf of God

Roman Empire An ancient empire that stretched from Italy to as far away as Britain, Germany, and northern Africa. In 395, it split into two empires, the Western Roman Empire, which fell in 475, and the Byzantine Empire.

Soviet Having to do with, or a citizen of, the Union of Soviet Socialist Republics (U.S.S.R.), or Soviet Union, which existed from 1922 to 1991

veteran A person who was once in the armed forces, especially someone who fought in a war

worship To honor or respect a god

Index

2 3 4 5 6 7 8 9 0 Printed in the USA 5 4 3